focus
on the moment
and
trust
in God's love

Read it forward - live it backwards

by Gene P. Neral

Copyright © 2023 Gene P. Neral.

All rights reserved. No part of this book may be reproduced, stored, or transmitted by any means—whether auditory, graphic, mechanical, or electronic—without written permission of both publisher and author, except in the case of brief excerpts used in critical articles and reviews. Unauthorized reproduction of any part of this work is illegal and is punishable by law.

Unless otherwise indicated, Scripture Quotations taken from the New American Bible. Copyright © 1990, 2006 Published by Oxford University Press 198 Madison Ave., New York, NY 10016. Used by permission. All rights reserved.

ISBN: 979-8-89031-390-4 (sc)
ISBN: 979-8-89031-391-1 (hc)
ISBN: 979-8-89031-392-8 (e)

Because of the dynamic nature of the Internet, any web addresses or links contained in this book may have changed since publication and may no longer be valid. The views expressed in this work are solely those of the author and do not necessarily reflect the views of the publisher, and the publisher hereby disclaims any responsibility for them.

One Galleria Blvd., Suite 1900, Metairie, LA 70001
(504) 702-6708
1-888-421-2397

My prayer
for each person who reads this book
is that, with the help of what it contains,
you will respond
to **the grace of each moment** in your life
as you receive it.

This work is dedicated
to our Lord Jesus Christ,
who, with His Divine Providence,
has directed my life
in ways I could never have imagined;
to our Blessed Mother,
who, with her love and protection,
has been with me constantly;
to Great Saint Joseph,
my spiritual father and protector;
and
to my wife, Barbara,
who has loved, supported,
and been extremely patient with me
for over fifty-eight years
of our married life.

CONTENTS

Acknowledgments ix

Foreword xi

Introduction xvii

Chapter 1 Recovery and Discovery 1

Chapter 2 When God Has a Plan 12

Chapter 3 God Prepares,
           We are Unaware 24

Chapter 4 Read It Forward;
           Live It Backwards 32

Chapter 5 Trusting God with
           Everything 40

Chapter 6 "Focus on the Moment" 53

Chapter 7 Our Blessed Mother
           Said "YES" 68

Chapter 8   A Gift from Saint Thérèse.... 81

Chapter 9   More Gifts from Our
            Lady and Saint Joseph.......... 86

Chapter 10 Feedback from Those Cards .. 92

Conclusion 101

Bibliography 109

ACKNOWLEDGMENTS

JMJ

I also wish to acknowledge: Leslie McCurdy, who helped design the ministry card which contains the phrase explained in this work; Rev. Fr. Silvan Rouse C.P., who helped me to discover the true meaning of the words of that phrase; my family, my spiritual directors, those who helped with the editing, all who encouraged and prayed for me throughout this endeavor; and Allen J. Capriotti, whose inspiring mural helped me to develop the conclusion of this work.

FOREWORD

JMJ

TRUST GOD! TAKE THINGS ONE DAY AT A TIME! These are things we hear and say all the time when life seems uncertain or when things just don't seem to be going the way we want. We become anxious with ourselves and anxious with God.

Deacon Gene Neral offers thought-provoking and practical guidance on how we need to put these two components of living our faith together in a life filled with uncertainty. He challenges us to take one moment at a time,

focus on the moment and trust in God's Love

focus upon what is before us, and accept the grace of each moment as we receive it.

What makes this difficult is that we do not include the total element of trust in God as we focus. Trusting in God's love is a prerequisite for focusing with faith. Without first having trust in God's love and care for us, focusing on the moment is extremely difficult and often not possible.

Deacon Gene draws on his own personal life, relationship with God, and spirituality to demonstrate how he learned this lesson. He also draws on the lives of saints and the Blessed Mother, in a way that enables us to understand his simple message through the eyes of "Abandonment to Divine Providence."

In his book, Deacon Gene puts it all together by giving us a very simple principle to remember every day:

*"focus on the moment and
trust in God's love."*
"Read it forward – live it backwards."

*Father Tony Legarski
Diocese of Altoona-Johnstown*

focus on the moment and trust in God's Love

Deacon Gene writes with an innocence and realism that reaches to the core of our relationship with God. His life experiences and conversations with the Lord bring us to the realization that our loving God is constantly revealing Himself to us and invites us to open our minds and hearts so that we can be drawn closer to Him, the God who loved us first.

Deacon Gene's writing style draws the reader into his personal trials and struggles and his prayerful communications with the Lord. It is a blessing that he shares these intimate moments with us so that we too may seek and find the Lord at every turn in our lives and abandon ourselves to His Divine Providence.

Foreword

This book should be read slowly so that the reader can appreciate the power of God entering our lives and through that appreciation understand that God is always seeking us, waiting for us at every life event, to turn to Him for grace, mercy, and guidance.

Deacon Michael Russo, Obl. S.B., M.A.
Director of the Office of the
Permanent Diaconate
Diocese of Altoona-Johnstown, PA

God's plan for each of us is that we become saints. Sanctity, therefore, is within everyone's reach. In his book, Deacon Gene Neral relates through his own experiences how, with God's grace, we can cooperate *moment by moment* in striving to fulfill that plan. The key is to focus on the moment, one at a time, and to trust with unbounded confidence that God's love will lead the way.

focus on the moment and trust in God's Love

Devotees of St. Thérèse and St. Faustina will find in these pages a wealth of inspiration that reinforces their already foundational reliance on God's merciful love. All, however, can benefit from the spiritual gems that can lead to a deeper, loving relationship with God.

Mother John of the Cross, O.C.D., Prioress
Discalced Carmelite Nuns
Carmel of Saint Thérèse of Lisieux,
Loretto, PA

INTRODUCTION

JMJ

When people read the nine words that make up the title of this work, one of the responses that I have often heard is, "I needed that"; another is, "I like that!"

At first glance, the meaning seems quite clear, but when given a little more thought or explanation, the full meaning contained in those words can be a life-changing revelation. That has been my experience with these words, as you will see as you read on in this book.

focus on the moment and trust in God's Love

In the pages that follow, I hope to explain the meaning of that phrase and why you have to learn to live it backwards, even though you read it forward.

My prayer for each person who reads this book is that you will respond to ***the grace of each moment*** in your life, ***as you receive it,*** and learn to ***live each moment*** with ***complete TRUST in GOD'S LOVE.***

We may not all make an earth-shattering discovery in our lifetime, but we may from time to time make smaller discoveries that can change the direction of our life. The key to making discoveries is to keep searching, and the key to finding the answers to the most difficult questions is to keep asking.

Sometimes we have to search for or ask the same question a number of times, and when the answer comes, it may be in a way we just don't expect. **There are also times when we don't even know the question, much less the answer.**

When it comes to questions of faith and growth in our spiritual life, what we have to realize is that **God speaks to us when, where, and how He chooses,** and the answers **He gives** to our questions **are always the right ones.**

That realization came to me one time through what some might consider my addiction, which is probably to westerns or movies about horses. I have been attracted to horses ever since I saw a black quarter horse in a rodeo when I was a young boy. For a long time, I really wished I could own one. At the age of seventy-three, I was still able to ride, but because of medical issues, that is no longer an option.

About forty years ago, I was watching a movie on television. It was part of a series called ***How the West Was Won.*** The episode began with a cowboy helping a widow and her young son retrieve the ferry that they used to transport people across the river in front of their cabin. It had been cut loose by some unruly neighbors. It took some time for the cowboy and the woman to restore the ferry to service on the river. But in the meantime, the life of the young boy became the focus of the story in a couple of ways.

For me, **the most interesting part of the movie was the young boy,** who seemed to have a learning disability and was very carefully protected by his mother. Evidently, a time before this episode occurred, the boy found a knife, which he knew his mother would take from him, so he hid it. Without her knowledge, he would go out into the woods, find a piece of wood, and begin to whittle. During the two-hour movie, the boy's mother was made aware of the fact that the boy had a knife, but **did not realize that he had developed a special gift.**

Toward the end of the story, the cowboy was ready to go on his way. The young boy had grown to like the cowboy and wanted to give him a parting gift. He went out into the woods, picked up some of his carvings, and wrapped them in a towel, and brought them to the ferry where the cowboy and his mother were waiting. As a special gift for the cowboy, he unwrapped one, which startled both of them. To their amazement, they saw a carving of two horses standing on their back legs, on a pedestal, **carved out of one piece of wood.**

When his mother saw it, she asked the boy, "Where did you get that?"

The boy replied, "I whittled it." Unable to immediately recognize the boy's special gift, the mother responded, "Did you do that with the knife you found?"

He replied, "Yes!"

In amazement, she asked, "Well, how did you do that?"

He replied, **"It's easy.** You go out into the woods, find a piece of wood with two horses in it, **then you whittle away at it until the horses come out."**

After hearing that, the story stopped for me. In my heart, I heard the Lord profoundly speak to me. He said, **"That is what I did for you. When you were baptized, I put the image of my Son in you. Then, down through the years, I have whittled away at all the excesses in your life to let the image of my Son come out."** How could I have missed that gift in my life for so long?

Even though it was late in the evening, I sat down and immediately wrote down my thoughts so I wouldn't forget. The image is so embedded in my mind that I have shared this story with many people over the years, getting the same reaction from all of them. **WOW!**

focus on the moment and trust in God's Love

As I pondered that story in the light of this work, it occurred to me that there might be another parallel to it. Just like many of us, even Saint Paul didn't immediately recognize the gift of God in his life. He was focused on what 'he' thought he should be doing. Since he was a devout Jew, he thought he should fight against the message those Christians were spreading throughout the known world. So, just like with all of us, God had to get his attention. Jesus knocked him to the ground with a blinding flash of light, then spoke to him about the real job he was to be doing and how he was to progress. For some of us, it may take just a tap on the shoulder. For others, like me, God may decide to use something like a 2x4 with a little more impact!

Introduction

I can remember lying in my hospital bed at Hershey Medical Center, recuperating from my third brain tumor operation in ten years and asking God why I had to keep going through this. Actually, I got a response that I didn't expect.

In my heart, I heard Him ask me, **"Do I have your attention yet?"**

Of course, I said, **"YES,"** thinking I knew what He was asking me. When I had another tumor two years later, I realized that I must have a short attention span, or else I just wasn't listening well enough. God may not be as obvious for us as he was for Saint Paul, but we have to keep our eyes open to the events in our life through which He speaks and our ears open to listen for His voice.

focus on the moment and trust in God's Love

Most importantly, we must recognize that God **has a plan for each of us**. He doesn't give us all the details, and He doesn't tell us when we will reach our goal, but He does give us one moment at a time to live to the best of our ability.

I have often said that if God told us at the beginning of each day what He had in store for us, many of us would either have a panic attack or just stay in bed. It's also said that God only gives us one moment at a time because He knows that's all we can handle. This moment is a gift of God's merciful love, and how we handle His gift, as He gives it to us, can change our lives.

Through the first forty-one years of my life, I experienced opportunities and trials as well as the comfort of a wonderful family and a really good education. During the first twenty years of my working life, I tried a number of jobs and career opportunities, one of which even placed me in the position of trying to help others to be goal-directed and self-motivated in their lives.

Then, in the fall of 1981, something caused me to look deeper into the attitudes I had developed and the results of my efforts. I wasn't knocked to the ground, but I was involved in a head-on car collision.

What happened from then on, which I will explain in more detail in the first chapter of this book, brought me to the discovery of the phrase which you see as the title of this work.

Please note that in this whole work, when there is an opportunity for a lesson to be learned, as much as possible, **it is written in the first person.** This is done intentionally in the hope that each person who reads these pages may be able to ponder the message in the deepest recesses of his or her own heart.

For example: I need to recognize that whatever I experience in reading this work will differ from what anyone else experiences, because I am different; I am unique. I am the only one who can receive what God has in store specifically for me because He made me that way. I may also ask, "How do I know when I've gotten everything I can from this work?" Only God Knows! Chances are, if I read it more than once, I may discover new insights, because, based on what I have experienced, each day begins with new questions and new answers from a new me.

1. RECOVERY AND DISCOVERY

> *J M J*

As I mentioned, I was involved in a head-on collision while driving. Recovering from that took weeks. Because of the whiplash from the accident, my neck stiffened, and weeks of treatment didn't seem to alleviate the problem. Eventually, as part of my treatment, one of the doctors suggested that I have a CT-scan of my head. The afternoon of the scan, before they had an opportunity to review the results, my neck injury began to improve. However, when they reviewed the scan, the doctors discovered that I had a brain tumor at the intersection of my optic nerve. It was a "skull-based meningioma" and was removed through invasive surgery in January 1982. Thank God it was benign!

Since then, I have had three more occurrences of the same tumor in the same place, two of which were removed with invasive surgery. The last one, which appeared in the fall of 1993, was treated using what is known as a "Gamma Knife" procedure, using lasers, developed in Sweden.

During that period from 1982 to 1993, I had the opportunity to reassess my life and my options. Since the early 1970s, and through my ministry as a deacon, beginning in 1985, I had tried to help people improve their way of life through seminars and talks. I thought I was using the right words, but it was amazing how few people seemed to understand what I was trying to teach them and how little it affected my own life. Something had to change, and it did.

Since December of 1991, I have been sharing, with anyone who will listen, the phrase that you saw on the front cover of this work,

focus
on the moment
and
trust
in God's love

This little phrase came together for me in the spring, summer, and fall of 1991. While still recuperating from my second brain tumor operation in April of 1991, I was talking with my co-worker, Leslie McCurdy, about my inability to get my message across. I remember telling her, "I need to get people to focus." The word "***focus***" hit me so hard, I asked her to write it down. She made a sign with that word, just as you see it, tacked it on my bulletin board, and taped it on the window of my office. I began talking to people about putting their life in "***focus.***" I soon realized that people were telling me all about what happened in the past and what they would like to experience in the future, but few, if any, seemed to be ready to talk about what was happening in their life NOW. It became apparent that people really needed to learn to "***focus on the moment.***" We immediately changed the little sign on my bulletin board and my window, and I began to speak to people about what it means to "***focus on the moment.***"

Recovery and Discovery

In October of that year, I was told that my tumor had returned and that I would have to have another surgery. Shortly after informing all of my co-workers that I would be going into the hospital again, I was talking with one of them about ***"focusing on the moment."*** Since he had just heard about my impending surgery, he gave me the time-out sign and asked, "How can you ***'focus on the moment'*** when someone is going to cut your head open in another month?" I replied, ***"You just have to trust in God's love."*** We immediately realized that we had to add that thought to the signs we had posted. While undergoing my third tumor surgery, Leslie had fold-over cards printed up for me.

They read,

focus on the moment
and
trust in God's love

She sent them with my wife, Barbara, who was returning to visit me at Hershey Medical Center.

As soon as I was able to get out of bed, I began to put those little cards on the nurses' carts and leave one on the bedside table of patients I was able to visit. I was amazed at how many people were able to identify with the words on that little card and responded favorably. For over twenty-nine years now, I have given one of those cards to almost everyone who would give me a chance to at least introduce myself. As I present each card, I try to explain how living with this truth in mind can make a difference in a person's life.

Besides being blessed with God-fearing parents; a loving wife; three great sons, the youngest of whom has already gone to his eternal reward; their wives; four grandchildren; and my Catholic Faith, the discovery of this phrase has been the biggest influence in my life. **I was even convinced I knew what it meant and had tried to make it the motto for my ministry as a Permanent Deacon in the Catholic Church.**

Then in the spring of 1995, I began a relationship with a Passionist priest (professed members of a Roman Catholic religious institute founded by Saint Paul of the Cross with special emphasis on the Passion of Jesus Christ) who agreed to become my spiritual director. During a July visit with Fr. Silvan, my newfound confidant and guide, I began to explain my interpretation of that little card. He broke in and said, "That came from Abandonment to Divine Providence." I asked what he meant, and he replied, "That idea came from a book called **Abandonment to Divine Providence** by Jean-Pierre de Caussade,[1] a Jesuit priest who lived in the seventeenth and early eighteenth centuries."

I said, "Father, that phrase came to me while working through several surgeries for a recurring brain tumor. I don't know anything about a book." I didn't have the heart to put him through the ordeal of explaining all that

---

[1] Jean-Pierre de Caussade, *Abandonment to Divine Providence* (New York: Doubleday, 1975).

had happened in my life the previous thirty years, but I explained enough that enabled him to realize I was still puting forth a lot of effort in coping with life as I encountered it and that I was open to further explanations.

He asked me to read the book. Within the next month, I bought it and read it from cover to cover. On my next visit with Father Silvan, in August, I told him that I didn't quite understand. I asked him how that seventeenth-century priest knew what I was going to say four hundred years later. He simply replied, "With God, there's nothing new. You just discovered it in your life."

That discovery occurred because I kept searching and questioning those to whom I looked for guidance. The priest who opened that door for me, Father Silvan Rouse, C.P., who has since gone to his eternal reward, showed me an unbelievable amount of understanding and compassion.

Then on a June evening in 1997, I had a lengthy conversation with a Holy Ghost Father (a priest) from Nairobi, Kenya, who was visiting my home parish of St. John the Evangelist on a mission appeal.

Of course, my little card became part of that discussion, and he told me that he taught a course on the book ***Abandonment to Divine Providence*** but that he had never heard it explained my way. He told me that there were probably a lot of people who could benefit from my experiences if I could figure out how to identify them. He said one of the best ways to do that would be with a book. When I told him that I had no idea of how to write a book, he spent the next hour and a half giving me some guidelines on how to begin. The next morning, he spent an hour reviewing some of what you just read. He was pleased with my initial effort and encouraged me to continue.

I have since lost touch with him, and, as you can see by the timing of this work, it took quite a while for me to muster the courage, find the help that I needed, and gain the confidence in God's blessings to share these ideas which are so close to my heart. What follows is my attempt to finish what he motivated me to start.

2. WHEN GOD HAS A PLAN

[J M J]

Sometimes it helps to tell a story from the beginning. My elementary school years were spent at Immaculate Conception School in Johnstown, PA. Initially, that may seem insignificant, but when I think about what has occurred in recent years, it becomes clear that it was all part of God's plan for my life. The growth in my faith goes back to those years where I was taught by ***The Sisters of Divine Providence.*** That was where I was first introduced to the gift of God's Divine

Providence. It was a gift of God's grace that I now consider to be the first step in a long journey of search and discovery.

My devotion to our Blessed Mother, Mary, under the title of ***the Immaculate Conception,*** can also be traced back to the sisters. I have worn a sterling silver ***"Miraculous Medal"*** since they gave it to me on May 9, 1948, the occasion of my First Holy Communion.

Upon graduation from grade school in 1954, I spent almost five years in training, with a view to the priesthood, with the **Society of Mary**, ***"Marianists."*** My high school years were spent in Beacon, NY. My novitiate was in Utica, NY, followed by college at the University of Dayton. In the spring of 1959, on a doctor's advice, that adventure in my life came to an abrupt end. Going through high school in three years and almost immediately starting novitiate and college courses was evidently too much for me to handle. In the spring of that fifth year, I went home.

Upon my return home to Johnstown, it seemed like it would take forever to get a good job. One day, some friends of my father from Lancaster, PA, offered a place to stay and an opportunity to look for work. By 10:00 a.m. the next morning, I had a job, and the next part of my life's journey began.

Since my faith has always been a big part of my life, as soon as I was able to lease an apartment, I began to look for a church. After a number of visits, I settled on Sacred Heart Parish in Lancaster. It would become my spiritual home and a church in which

I would later be married. In our opening conversation, I told the pastor that I liked to sing, so, immediately, after he had the information he needed, he took me over to the church and introduced me to the choir. It was there that I met Barbara (Ranck), who, two and a half years later, became my wife.

We were married in November of 1962 and, in the next five years, created our family, which included three sons—James William, David Michael, and Jeffrey Stephen, who has already gone to his eternal reward.

From 1962 to 1976, I had various employment opportunities and jobs, none of which proved to adequately fulfill our family's needs. Sometimes there were two jobs and sometimes three. Looking back, I realize that was God's way of saying He had other plans. After almost fourteen years of floundering, I got a real break. Due to a chance meeting with an advertising agency friend, I was introduced to the owners of a weekly newspaper group who were looking for an advertising salesperson. I accepted the job and was able to provide a stable income for my family for the next twenty-four years.

In the beginning of 2000, I retired after serving as the advertising salesman, sales manager, and general manager of that newspaper group, which had doubled in publications and increased its net worth fivefold during my tenure.

During the period from 1970 to now, my spiritual life has also undergone some major renovations.

In 1971, my pastor at Saint Ann Parish in Lancaster, where we had moved after our marriage, asked me to consider the idea of becoming a Permanent Deacon in the Catholic Church. When I questioned what he meant, he explained that the Church had reinstated the Diaconate as a Permanent Order and that it was available to married men. I told him I would be interested if he could explain how to proceed. He said that the first step was to write a letter to the bishop asking for acceptance into formation. Since I said that I didn't know the bishop, he agreed to write the letter. Although the program had not been started in the Harrisburg Diocese, on May 1, I received a letter from the Most Rev. Joseph T. Daley telling me that he would consider an application from me as soon as they began the program in that diocese.

focus on the moment and trust in God's Love

In 1973, an employment change took me to the Altoona- Johnstown Diocese, also in Pennsylvania. When I showed the Altoona-Johnstown Diocesan bishop my letter from Bishop Daley, Bishop Hogan said, "That's a nice letter, but we don't have that program yet."

By 1977, without any progress toward that vocation, I almost gave up the idea, when something marvelous happened. On the twenty-minute drive home from work one day, I had been telling God that it was alright if He didn't want me to be a Permanent Deacon. I was beginning to feel comfortable in what I was doing with the newspapers, and I was able to provide for my family. It was the first Friday in May, and our pastor, Fr. Regis Myers, at Saint Catherine of Siena Parish in Duncansville always had exposition of the Blessed Sacrament all day on the First Friday of each month. I decided to stop in at the church for a short visit before continuing home for dinner. I had a pocket-sized New Testament that I either carried with me or kept in the car. After a short time on my knees in prayer in front of the Blessed Sacrament, I decided to just sit and see what might come out of some quiet time. Then the thought came to me that some words from Scripture might be appropriate. I opened that New Testament, and I saw 2 Timothy 4:1-5.

There I was, sitting in the presence of Jesus exposed in the Monstrance on the altar, and this is what I read.

focus on the moment and trust in God's Love

I charge you in the presence of God and of Christ Jesus, who will judge the living and the dead, and by His appearing and His kingly power: proclaim the word, be persistent whether it is convenient or inconvenient; convince, reprimand, and encourage through all patience and teaching. For the time will come when people will not tolerate sound doctrine but, following their own desires and insatiable curiosity, will accumulate teachers and will stop listening to the truth and will be diverted to myths. But you, be self-possessed in all circumstances; put up with hardship; perform the work of an evangelist; fulfill your ministry.

As I have told many people since, I didn't know whether to stand and salute or just say "OK." But, from that moment on, I believed that I would one day be a Permanent Deacon in the Catholic Church. I didn't know how or when; I just knew I would.

In the meantime, at the suggestion of the bishop, I began to take some theology and related courses at Saint Francis Seminary in Loretto, PA. At the end of the second semester, I had an interesting encounter with the rector of the Seminary. He approached and asked me if I was studying to be a priest. I told him that I had a wife and three sons and that I was trying to follow the bishop's recommendation to begin studies toward becoming a deacon of the Church. He suggested that we should have a talk with the bishop, which we did, and together, we decided that it would be more appropriate to wait until the program of Diaconate Formation was formally introduced in the Diocese.

Almost five years after my encounter with Jesus at Saint Catherine's, I received an invitation from the Most Rev. James J. Hogan of the Diocese of Altoona-Johnstown to participate in information sessions to discuss the idea of beginning studies toward becoming a Permanent Deacon in the Catholic Church. As part of the first class of five Permanent Deacons for the Diocese, I was ordained on June 1, 1985.

In the past thirty-five years, I was assigned to one parish for ten years and a second for over twenty-five years. During that time, I have assisted three bishops in liturgical ministry and was the master of ceremonies for the last two bishops on a number of occasions. I also spent eleven of those years as Director of the Permanent Diaconate for our diocese. I retired from that position in January of 2015, with the help of Deacon Michael L. Russo, who first took over the Formation Process and eventually agreed to accept the appointment as Director of the Diaconate. I continue in my assignment as Deacon for St. John the Evangelist Parish in Lakemont, Altoona, PA, where I have served since July of 1995.

3. GOD PREPARES, WE ARE UNAWARE

> JMJ

Getting back to that little card that I wrote about in the first chapter, I have to mention that God's guiding hand in the discovery of that phrase on my little card became clearer to me in the spring of 2008. Barbara and I sold the house we built twenty-two years before and prepared to move into an apartment designed for those fifty-five and older. In the midst of the task of downsizing and packing up the balance of my library, I found journals in which I kept notes from retreats I made in 1984, 1986, and 1988. I usually made notes while on retreat that seem even more significant now than they did at the time.

The journals were notes from retreats at **Bethlehem Hermitage** in Chester, New Jersey, and ***The Center for Divine Mercy*** in Stockbridge, MA. My notes began on May 7, 1984 (one year before my ordination to the Diaconate), while on retreat at ***Bethlehem Hermitage.***

For those who are not familiar with the term, a hermitage is a place of religious seclusion where a person can spend time in quiet, mostly in prayer and meditation. Bethlehem is a center with a series of 16'x16' cabins in the midst of about sixty acres of trees, where a person can spend a week in solitude. For more information: http://www.bethlehemhermits.org.

On my first visit to the hermitage, my cabin was under the patronage of Saint Joseph. As you will see at the end of chapter eight, ***now my whole life is dedicated to Saint Joseph.***

When I arrived, Father Eugene Romano, who is the Desert Father of the Hermits of Bethlehem, told me that he would assist me if I could not come up with a theme for my retreat. I told him that I just wanted to spend some quiet time to possibly hear the voice of God and know it was Him speaking to me.

I arrived at my cabin in the woods and thought I would take a break and lie down, but I noticed that someone had tacked a brown-paper bag on the wall on which were written the words: ***"This is what God asks of you, only this... to act justly, to love tenderly and to walk humbly with your God"*** (Mic. 6:8). Instantly, I had a theme for my retreat. In fact, I wrote in my journal, **"If I could fulfill that request in its entirety, it would change my life."**

Amazingly, two weeks after my return home from that retreat, I received a card in the mail from someone, the front of which reads: ***"This is what God asks of you, only this... to act justly, to love tenderly and to walk humbly with your God"*** (Mic. 6:8). There was no signature or return address. To me, it was confirmation that I had picked the right theme for my retreat, and that card has remained on a shelf in my prayer corner for over thirty-six years.

focus on the moment and trust in God's Love

Reflecting on that retreat, I believe God first spoke to my heart when I was about fourteen years old. Thinking at the time I was too young, I followed, not knowing exactly where I was going or when I would get there. My commitment was not total, and my reasons were very shallow. I really didn't know what it meant to be called by God. Maybe that is why my early experience of religious life ended so abruptly. As I look back now, I can see that there was a reason for my undergoing the kind of training that I received even though my initial efforts may have been very inadequate.

Over the years, I continued to tell God that I was too young, too weak, and too inadequate, that I didn't have the experience or education. Each time, He seemed to give me another opportunity to improve even when my response had been halfhearted. He keeps prodding me and putting me in situations that cause me to grow.

As I knelt before the Blessed Sacrament one afternoon in May 1984, I believed and made notes that "I know God wants me to do something, just as sure as I know I'm supposed to be here this week." My questions were what and when, but that obviously indicates that I was experiencing a lack of trust in God's providence.

I began to tell the Lord that I am not worthy, am totally inadequate, and have such little love. He seemed to interrupt my thinking to say, "I am worthy, I am adequate, I am love. You say that you want to love; I am love. You say you want wisdom; I am wisdom. You say that you want to be able to speak a word of truth to My people; I am the Word made Flesh; I am the truth and the life. You say that you want to help bring salvation to the world; I am the Savior of the world. Why don't you just come to Me, be absorbed in Me, and let Me use you as My instrument, to achieve My will in My own time?" Two years later, during my second retreat, this thought became clearer.

Even now, when I read the challenge I received in 1977 in St. Paul's second letter to Timothy, it seems to me that I am dreaming because I am not worthy of the calling to the Permanent Diaconate in the Church.

However, one lesson that I learned is that our God is so great that He is able to transform me without destroying me. He is able to give me wisdom without over-powering me, and He is able to trans-figure me into the image of His Son while allowing me to maintain my individuality and use the unique talents and abilities He has given me. That's because He wants me to become the unique individual He created me to be.

4. READ IT FORWARD; LIVE IT BACKWARDS

JMJ

Before continuing with this story, it may help to consider that not one of us has received a gift from God that is meant to be put on a mantle to be admired by those around us. Whatever we have received from God, whether it is a gift of time, talent, or treasure, according to Saint Paul **(in Eph. 4:11, 12),** is given "for building up the Body of Christ." Hopefully, as you continue with this book, you will see how I am trying to share some gifts that I believe God has given me for the upbuilding of the community.

The next steps of my discovery became clearer during my second retreat at the Bethlehem Hermitage. Consider the phrase on the front cover of this book:

focus
   on the moment
       and
trust
   in God's love

After reading the book ***Abandonment to Divine Providence,*** as I mentioned in chapter one, my spiritual director, Fr. Silvan Rouse, taught me a very important lesson. He told me that according to the author, Père de Caussade, even though I read the phrase that I had written from left to right, top to bottom, I had to learn to **live it in reverse**. He explained that first, I have to believe that **God loves me**. Then I have to learn to **TRUST God** with everything I am and everything I have. **Then and only then can I focus on the moment, do my best, and TRUST that God will do the rest.**

Most of us were taught as little children, "God loves you." But it wasn't until I learned that ***"God loves ME"*** that it began to make a real difference.

While on the second retreat in ***Bethlehem Hermitage,*** Fr. Romano decided to help me with the theme for my retreat. He gave me a number of passages to read, for my meditations, from the ***Old*** and the ***New Testaments*** of the ***Bible.*** They were all about ***God's love.*** The more I read, the more I recognized the presence of God in my little cabin. At one point, on Wednesday afternoon, my cabin became so full of God's love that I felt I would suffocate if I didn't get out and take a walk. Throughout the sixty or so acres of trees on the hermitage grounds, there were a number of paths. I began to walk down one of them, noticing the different sizes and shapes of those many trees. Then a still, small voice in my heart said, ***"They are here because I love you."*** A little further along, a squirrel crossed my path, and that voice spoke again: ***"It's here because I love you."*** In a couple of minutes, a small herd of deer, about six or seven of them, crossed my path, and in my heart, I heard, ***"They're here because I love you."***

focus on the moment and trust in God's Love

Eventually, I arrived at the entrance of the hermitage where there is a twenty-foot-high wooden cross that greets all those who enter. When I looked up at it, that voice in my heart said, ***"It's here because I love you."***

After a long pause, I began the walk back to my cabin. Immediately, I noticed a number of other hermits, people who were on retreat at the same time, walking through the woods. They could be seen, but no communication occurred or was permitted. Again, I heard that voice in my heart: ***"They are here because I love you."*** Then, to my surprise, I also heard, ***"You're here because I love them."***

I thought, "That is amazing!" They are here because God loves me, and I am here because God loves them. That also means that you are here because God loves me and I am here because God loves you.

Does that leave anybody out? Absolutely not! The whole universe is here for one reason. God loves us, and His plan is for us to love one another. That is the marvel of it all. If we could learn to live with this truth in mind, the whole world would change.

Back at the cabin, I saw a little paper on the desk. It said, "I have come to set the earth on fire, and how I wish it were already blazing" (***Luke 12:49).*** The more I thought about it, the more it became clear that the fire in that phrase is the fire of God's love. And I realized how much God must want me to be part of that fire. All of a sudden, I felt like a stranger in a foreign land. I thought about how far I must be from where God wants me to be. Then it occurred to me that the world does not know what the fire of God's love is. Therefore, when that fire begins burning in the lives of God's people, ***the world tries to put it out***. What we have to realize is that ***we have to fan the flame of God's love in our life.***

The question then came to mind: ***"How does the fact that I now know God loves ME play out in my life?"*** Needless to say, the answer indicated that I had a lot of work to do. It's one of the questions **we all have to ask** but may not be too quick to answer for fear it points out our weaknesses in living God's law of love.

As I browsed through the notes from my retreats, I realized that God had been trying to tell me something and had allowed an interesting scenario to unfold in my life over those eleven years between the retreats and meeting my spiritual director in 1995.

According to my notes, it was a couple of years, another retreat, and the guidance of my spiritual director, Fr. Silvan, before God was able to break through with me regarding the essential element of ***TRUST*** in His message.

5. TRUSTING GOD WITH EVERYTHING

> JMJ

Although I began to see that God loves me, I still didn't understand how important the element of trust is to a life of abandonment to Divine Providence.

A lesson that I eventually learned from my spiritual director, Fr. Silvan, was that on my card, the original emphasis on the word *focus* was out of proportion to the word *trust,* which is actually the most important word. It is only **after** I am willing to ***TRUST*** God with everything I am and everything I have that

I can *focus on the moment*, do my best, and *trust* that God will do the rest. Subsequent printings of the card show that the word *trust* is the most important.

I have often heard people use the expression "I put my trust in God." But do they really mean that they ***"TRUST God"***? Saying, "I put my trust in God," or, "In God we trust," are just expressions, but to ***TRUST God*** with everything I am and everything I have is an act of faith and of one's will. Jesus once asked His disciples if when the Son of Man comes He will find any faith on the earth. Will He also find people who are willing to ***TRUST*** Him to the end?

If Jesus were to come back right now, and everyone in the world **doubted Him** but me, who would be the winner? If He came back

focus on the moment and trust in God's Love

now and everyone in the world **believed in Him** except me, who would be the loser? If I start with the premise that God loves me and trust in His assurance that He called me into this life by name and that I am His, then I am really just acknowledging the fact that everything I have and everything I am is already His as well. Where most of us run into problems is when we begin to think that the **things** we have been able to accumulate and **the talents and abilities we have been able to develop** somehow **belong to us.** That was surely my problem.

A person who was very instrumental in my understanding of that truth was Helena Kowalska, who became *Sister Maria Faustina of the Most Blessed Sacrament* and since April 2000 has been recognized in the Church as ***Saint Maria Faustina.*** My knowledge of her began in 1988 when I spent a week at the Shrine of Divine Mercy in Stockbridge, Massachusetts, for the third of my journaled retreats.

As with previous retreats, the notes from my journal helped me to recognize God's promptings.

A week that began as a rather routine experience turned into one of the most enlightening times of my life. The director of the Divine Mercy center, who had intended to be my retreat master, was unexpectedly called to Rome. In his absence, another priest of the house, Fr. George Kosicki, agreed to direct my retreat. At the time, I didn't know anything about Fr. George or the fact that he was so prominent in the promotion of

focus on the moment and trust in God's Love

the ***Devotion to the Divine Mercy*** because I was just in the process of discovering the devotion itself.

One of the first problems Fr. George said he recognized in me was that I am always trying to direct, lead, and understand instead of learning how to follow. He finished one of our first discussions with a Latin phrase that he said came from Saint Ignatius of Loyola: **"agere contra"** (against one's self or nature). He translated it, **"Do the opposite,"** or, **"When you feel you need to be in control, that is exactly when you should be letting go."** He suggested that one of the best ways to learn this lesson was to go into the chapel and sit before Jesus in the Blessed Sacrament and just be present. Just put yourself in the arms of Jesus and His Blessed Mother and ask them to take over. So that's what I did.

I went into the Divine Mercy Chapel. There before me was a statue of our Blessed Mother, the picture of the Divine Mercy, the image of Jesus on the Cross, and Jesus in the Blessed Sacrament reserved in the Tabernacle. As I gazed at the statue of Mary, I wanted to tell her how beautiful she is and how I longed to be worthy of being her son. In my heart, I heard her say to me, "Look at the image of my Son hanging on the cross and learn about suffering and mercy. We will have all eternity to speak about love and beauty." Each time I moved my head to gaze at her statue, she seemed to be telling me to keep my eyes fixed on the cross and learn the true meaning of suffering.

It was as if she were saying that I could only be called her son in so far as I allowed her to fashion me in the image of that most precious Son of hers who hung on the cross for my sins. In my heart, I felt her pulling me to take her hand and allow her to lead me to where I should go. I felt her speaking to me and telling me that in her glorified state, she could gaze on her Divine Son in the glory of His Resurrected Body and direct me to Him, but that it would be impossible for me to find the way myself. I knew I didn't fully grasp the meaning of His gift of salvation through the cross, but if I continued to allow her to show me the way, I was confident it would lead me to Jesus in a way I had never known before.

From that moment on, each time I went into the chapel, I spent about fifteen to twenty minutes just being present. I told Fr. George about all the time I was spending in the chapel and that I really didn't feel much different. He said that "feeling" was not the important thing; being present was essential. By Thursday afternoon at five o'clock, I had been thinking for about an hour how much I would like to go home. However, in the past, when I had felt that way during a retreat but stayed and finished, God managed to give me a special grace. God knew that I needed to stay, and I was not disappointed.

The Diary of Sister M. Faustina Kowalska: Divine Mercy in My Soul[2] and the words of Fr. George Kosicki helped me realize the importance of what Father Silvan would explain to me a number of years later. First,

---

[2] Kowalska, M. Faustina, SMDM. *The Diary of the Servant of God Sister M. Faustina Kowalska: Divine Mercy in My Soul* (Stockbridge, MA: Marian Press, 1987).

believe that **God loves me.** Then learn to **TRUST God with everything I am and everything I have.** At that time, I didn't understand the full message. But the inspiration of Faustina's words and the image of Jesus, which He asked her to paint, with the saying at the bottom, **"Jesus, I trust in you,"** made a lasting impression.

When I returned home and had an opportunity to speak to my pastor, I shared with him what I learned from the writings of Sister Faustina and from my time with Fr. George. I told him of my desire to spread the word about *Divine Mercy* and how important it is to **TRUST** in **God's love.** He asked me what I wanted to do. I told him that the first thing we should do is get a picture of *The Divine Mercy* for our parish.

Then we should celebrate the second Sunday of Easter each year with special devotions to the ***Divine Mercy.*** He agreed with both ideas, and we have now celebrated ***Divine Mercy Sunday*** at Saint Catherine of Siena Parish in Duncansville, PA, for over thirty years.

An amazing thing happened to me in the third year of that endeavor. Together with some friends, we made a donation to the sisters in Poland who are part of the religious order to which Sister Faustina belonged. We found out that they wanted to refurbish their convent in preparation for the beatification of Sister Faustina, and we wanted to help. About six months later, I received in the mail a first-class relic of Blessed Maria Faustina, which came to us with the faculty to be kept and to be exposed to the public veneration of the faithful, according to the norms of Canon Law. Every year since then, we have made the relic available for the veneration of those who come to our devotions on Divine Mercy Sunday.

In 1999, when we heard that Blessed Faustina was to be canonized, it was suggested that it didn't seem right for us to have the relic of a saint in the little reliquary that I had purchased for about $35. Through the generosity of the participants at that celebration, we were able to purchase a more suitable twenty-four-carat gold one and had the relic placed in it for our devotions in April 2000, the day Saint Maria Faustina was canonized.

Since 1989, the number of people who attend our devotions on Divine Mercy Sunday have

Trusting God with Everything

seemed to have decreased, and some of the attendees have been concerned. I explained to them that in the course of years since then, a growing number of parishes in our diocese have begun a similar type of devotion on the same day and some even at the same time. That means the number of people who are involved in the devotion had doubled and tripled more than once. All we have to do is **TRUST** that the Lord knows what He is doing through the intercession of Saint Maria Faustina and that He will continue to expand this Divine Mercy devotion in our diocese and throughout the world if we just persevere.

In the spring of 2016, after rereading the Diary of Saint Faustina, and completing a retreat in preparation for a ***Consecration to***

the Divine Mercy, many of us discovered that we still have much to learn and do if we truly believe in what we are celebrating and to more faithfully promote the love and mercy of our God.

6. "FOCUS ON THE MOMENT"

> JMJ

Although I have been sharing this message with people for over twenty-nine years, the *"focus on the moment"* part of the phrase on my little card seems to be the hardest to put into practice. That may be why this chapter of the book has been the hardest to complete. From time to time, after a discussion with my spiritual director, we even decided that I should **put the book temporarily on hold.** Each time, we decided that God had a lesson to teach me that I didn't get yet. Of course,

focus on the moment and trust in God's Love

God has many lessons to teach us all the time. But this last time, we were more concerned about my awareness of the significance of the present moment.

The best example of someone who lived each moment to the fullest was the Blessed Virgin Mary. We don't know anything about her early life. But if we consider the moment of the Annunciation by the Angel Gabriel (Luke 1:26-38), we have an idea of how fully committed Mary was to live each moment in tune with the will of God. Her immediate response to the message of Gabriel changed the world. Her willingness to say yes at that moment made it possible for the Holy Spirit to conceive the Son of God in her womb. That was the beginning of the implementation of God's plan for the salvation of the world. Studying the gospels, we see numerous examples of Mary's life in tune with the will of God.

Another person who impressed me with her awareness of the present moment was Saint Thérèse of Lisieux. In the Epilogue of her autobiography, **"The Story of a Soul,"** we read, *"If I did not simply live from one moment to another, it would be impossible for me to be patient; but I only look at the present, I forget the past, and I take good care not to forestall the future. When we yield to discouragement or despair, it is usually because we think too much about the past and the future."*[3]

Saint Thérèse helps us to learn what it means to have faith and trust, even when we can't

---

[3] Therese. *Story of a Soul: the autobiography of St. Therese of Lisieux* (London: Burns, Oats & Washbourne, 1912). Pg. 203.

focus on the moment and trust in God's Love

see any evidence of what God is doing, and **to live each moment as God gives it to us.** She called this "***her little way.***"

A personal friend who actually helped me to understand what it means to live each moment was Sister Mary of Mount Carmel, OCD. She was an extern nun at the Carmelite Convent in Loretto, Pennsylvania. In other words, she was the one selected to greet everyone who came to Mass or to otherwise communicate with nuns in the cloister or the Mother Superior.

Everyone, including bishops, priests, deacons, and lay people, who visited were greeted with the same phrase: "Praised be Jesus Christ." We were expected to answer, "Now and forever." Then, regardless of why a person came, Sister Mary would first direct them to go to the chapel to say hello to Jesus, then she would help them with whatever else they had in mind.

Even our previous Bishop once said that she was the only person who ever told him where to go. Once, when he went to meet with the Mother Superior, he was met at the door by Sister Mary, who told him, "Go say hello to Jesus, and I will see if Mother is available."

By the way, I don't ever recall asking Sister Mary to recommend an intention of mine to the prayers of the nuns at Carmel that wasn't answered.

Even in the final years of her life (she died two months before her one-hundredth birthday), her awareness was astonishing. Even though she was confined to Garvey Manor Nursing

focus on the moment and trust in God's Love

Home, as she explained it, Jesus gave her a new job, to keep Him company in the chapel. She would be brought to the chapel for Mass in the morning, stay until noon, and have someone take her to her room for lunch, and then return to the chapel until about 4:00 p.m. One day, I happened to stop by to see her just about noon. I knelt down beside her, intending to stay a while before going out for my own lunch. However, Sister Mary turned to me and said, "Oh, Deacon Gene, I just asked Jesus to send someone to take me to lunch, and He sent you."

Needless to say, that caught me by surprise, but I will always remember how I was impressed by the fact that she had such an intimate relationship with Jesus. She could ask Jesus to send someone for her, and she expected Him to respond.

Because we are human and have been created in time, we experience time in our life. We remember things from the past and plan for things in the future. But what we remember from the past **is past,** and what we plan for the future **is not yet here** and may never be. The only time that we can do anything about is the time that we have **RIGHT NOW.**

Because our human minds were created in time, we struggle to grasp the idea of God's timeless existence. God is pure spirit and as such has no relationship to time. We describe Him as a God without beginning or end and say that He always was and always will be. That means that God is eternally **NOW!** So

focus on the moment and trust in God's Love

for us to be more fully in tune with God, we have to be **focused on NOW** as well.

Regularly during the months of May and October in our parish, we say the rosary before daily Mass. One morning, as we were praying, it occurred to me that in the second half of the Hail Mary, which we repeat over and over, we ask our Blessed Mother to **"pray for us sinners NOW and at the hour of our death."**

The more I repeated that petition, the more I pondered the fact that we were NOT asking Mary, our mother, to pray for us only when we are in trouble, when we need it, when she gets around to it, or when she happens to think about us. We keep asking her to **pray for us NOW!** That thought stuck with me through the end of the rosary and then, at least temporarily, left my mind.

Soon after, during the Mass, the gospel reading was about the marriage feast at Cana. When it came to the part that says, "His Mother said to the servers, 'Do whatever he tells you'" (John 2:5), the thought from the recitation of the rosary came back. If you think about it, you will realize that Mary didn't add or imply, "When you get around to it." Nor did she say, "When you feel like it," or, "When it's convenient." **Her implied NOW is obvious.**

When I gave additional thought to the sayings of Jesus in the gospels, **that implied NOW** seems to be more and more obvious. For instance, when Jesus told the disciples to love one another as He had loved them, He didn't add, "When you feel like it." When we consider the many healings that Jesus performed, **there was always an implied NOW in the commands of Jesus.**

When Jesus encountered the paralytic and told him that his sins were forgiven, He didn't say that they would be, but that they are (Mark 2:1 -12). When He told the man to pick up his mat and go home, **NOW was again obvious.**

The most dynamic instance of Jesus' "***focus on the moment***" and **implied NOW** occurred on Calvary. When He asked, **"Father, forgive them, they know not what they do."** (Luke 23:34) He expected that to happen immediately. That **NOW** has traveled down through the centuries and is still being applied to us today. It has been said many times, but is worth repeating, that Jesus is the same yesterday, today, and forever. His willingness to forgive us is also the same. So, the question is: how do I apply that **"*focus*"** and **implied NOW** to my daily life?

A request that has become part of my daily prayer is that God would give me the grace to respond to the gift **of each moment as He gives it to me.** When I attend Mass in the morning, I constantly ask our Lord to give me the grace to be attentive to His Word and fully participate in the Eucharist which is being celebrated. I want to be open to each of the many graces available at that time.

Will I be distracted? Will I be tempted by the duties of life and the responsibilities that go along with being human? Of course, I will.

focus on the moment and trust in God's Love

But we can all take the advice of Saint Teresa of Avila, who said that we are not to focus on the distractions but recognize them and return to the moment. Even in our prayer, where we are all distracted more than we would like to admit, the best action is to turn our attention back to the one with whom we are conversing. Saint Teresa admitted that she was plagued with distractions her entire life, but she still became a great saint.

One of the classic examples of distraction is recorded in the gospel account of Jesus walking on the water (Matt. 14:22-33). Recall that Peter asked Jesus to let him come to Him on the water. When Jesus told him to come, Peter was quick to get out of the boat. But when he felt how fierce the wind was and saw the waves at his feet, he was distracted from looking at Jesus and began to sink.

"Focus on the Moment"

There is a hymn called ***"Transfigure us, O Lord"* by Bob Hurd,**[4] which we often sing during Mass in our parish. There is a verse of that hymn that says, **"Where you lead, we'll follow, transfigure us, O Lord."** If we truly believe that the Lord Jesus **is leading us NOW,** then we need to continuously turn back to Him when other things distract us from His way. We have to **TRUST** that He will use each distraction as an opportunity for us to grow and each return as a reinforcement of our commitment to follow Him.

It takes such a burden off our life if we are willing to let the past be a memory and can anticipate with joy what God has in store for our future. Continually asking God to give us the grace to live each moment, as He gives it to

---

[4] Robert Hurd, *Breading Bread* "*Transfigure Us, O Lord* (Portland: OCP. 2020). #499.

us, helps us to come to grips with the fact that we can become a saint one moment at a time. I can start **RIGHT NOW** to become a saint. I can begin **NOW** to respond with thanksgiving to the gift of each moment as I receive it. I can't store up the graces I received yesterday, and I can't borrow from what I will receive tomorrow. But I can take full advantage of the grace of the present. The benefit I receive from the present grace prepares me to do my best with the next moment God is willing to give me. That is what saints do.

Remember what Jesus said, as we read in the gospel of Matthew 6:31-34:

> "So do not worry and say, 'What are we to eat?' or 'What are we to drink?' or 'What are we to wear?' All these things the pagans seek. Your heavenly Father

knows that you need them all. But seek *first* the kingdom [of God] and his righteousness, and all these things will be given you besides. Do not worry about tomorrow; tomorrow will take care of itself. Sufficient for a *day* is its own evil."

If we just substitute **"NOW"** for the word "*first*" and "*moment*" for the word "*day*," the **urgency of the present becomes more evident** in the words of Jesus.

As I said in the beginning, my prayer is that this book will assist **YOU** to **live each moment** of your life with **complete TRUST in GOD'S LOVE and** that **YOU** will respond to **the grace of each moment, as you receive it**. I include this same intention daily for every member of my family and for all the people who ask me to remember them in my prayers.

7. OUR BLESSED MOTHER SAID "YES"

JMJ

As I mentioned at the beginning of the previous chapter, from time to time, after a discussion with my spiritual director, we even decided that I should **put this book temporarily on hold.**

The last time that occurred was in the middle of September 2017.

At the end of the month, I was privileged to participate as the Deacon at Mass for the closing of the Solemn Novena in honor of

Saint Thérèse of Lisieux at the Carmelite Monastery in Loretto, PA. At the end of the closing night, it is customary for a group of young girls to pass out roses to all the participants.

My prayer for the week and especially on that Sunday to the Blessed Mother and to Saint Thérèse was a request. If they didn't want me to continue with this book, please give me **a red rose.** If it was OK for me to proceed with the book, I asked that I would receive **a yellow rose.**

At the end of the Mass, after the roses were given out and I didn't receive one, I proceeded to help by allowing people to venerate a relic of Saint Thérèse. When that was finished, I noticed that the baskets for the roses were empty, and I was resigned to not getting any.

Then one of the women who is in charge of hospitality for the event came up to me and said, "You need a rose," and handed me **a pale yellow rose**. She said, **"I tried to get you a red one, but they were all gone."** I immediately told her about my prayer, and we both rejoiced that **the only rose left was a yellow one**. I accepted that as a response to my prayer and immediately decided to go ahead with my plans for the book and **that rose, in dried form**, remains in my prayer corner even today.

As you will read shortly, that was not my first encounter with our Lady and her response with a pale yellow rose, but first, we have to go back a couple of years.

For quite a while, it has been my custom to walk the Stations of the Cross as often as I can each day. In the fall of 2015, as I was praying the Stations of the Cross after morning Mass at Saint John the Evangelist Parish, I came to the thirteenth station, and it suddenly touched me because of a unique difference that I never noticed before.

In contrast to Michelangelo's Pieta, in which Mary is looking down at Jesus in her lap, the image at this thirteenth station shows Mary with her hands folded and her eyes lifted in prayer to the Heavenly Father. When I looked at the image that day, it occurred to me that in the twelfth station, Jesus said to His Mother, "Woman, behold your son," and the next station is showing Mary, our Mother, praying for us.

When I went home, I went to my computer and wrote this:

focus on the moment and trust in God's Love

If we ponder this image and allow its meaning to touch our hearts, we may hear our Mother, Mary, in a petition to our Heavenly Father, saying, "Heavenly Father, please don't let the sufferings of my Son be in vain for your children. For the sake of His sorrowful passion, help them to put complete trust in His Merciful Love and dedicate their lives to satisfying His great thirst for their souls and for their love."

A few days later, as I was talking with my pastor, I showed him what I wrote, and he suggested that I should consider writing a new book, **in my words,** for the Stations of the Cross **as seen through the eyes of Mary.**

In May of 2016, after walking the Stations with Mary almost every day for about a year, I decided that it was time to write down what I was hearing our Blessed Mother say to my heart as I approached each station. I believe this is another gift that I have received from our Lady over the past couple of years.

The reception I received from people in my parish, some members of the clergy, and my friends, encouraged me. Although printing the Stations for groups of parishioners to use is under consideration, instead of waiting to have it put into book form, I decided to include it in my website for individual use. Since the new website is designed for a cell phone, walking the Stations of the Cross with a cell phone is especially easy and should be spiritually rewarding for anyone who tries it.

The link to the site is: http://www.lifeinfocus.net/ stations_of_the_cross.html.

While I was learning to walk the stations with her, but before I wrote what I was hearing, our Blessed Mother allowed me to experience another special gift.

On February 10, 2016, which, I didn't realize at the time, was **the Vigil of the Feast of Our Lady of Lourdes,** as I finished the **Chaplet of Mercy,** it occurred to me that I was not aware of a **chaplet for our Mother of Mercy.**

Immediately, the thought came to me that all the pieces were available, so I could put one together and then ask our Lady if she liked it. I went to my computer, pulled up a WORD document, and put together what seemed to work.

My Chaplet for **our Mother of Mercy** begins with: The Sign of the Cross. As with the Chaplet of Mercy, with which many people are familiar, on the string of three beads following we say **the Our Father, a Hail Mary, and the Apostles Creed.** Then, on the next (Our Father) bead, we say:

> **Hail, holy Queen, Mother of mercy, hail, our life, our sweetness, and our hope. To thee do we cry, poor banished children of Eve: to thee do we send up our sighs, mourning and weeping in this valley of tears. Turn then, most gracious Advocate, thine eyes of mercy toward us, and after this our exile, show unto us the**

blessed fruit of thy womb, Jesus, O clement, O loving, O sweet Virgin Mary; pray for us, O Holy Mother of God, that we may be made worthy of the promises of Christ! Amen.

On the strings of beads, ten times, we say, **"O Queen, Mother of Mercy, pray for us."** Then on the (Our Father) bead we repeat the "Hail Holy Queen."

After repeating that sequence five times, we finish with:

> **Remember, O most gracious Virgin Mary,** (help me to remember)**, that never was it known that anyone who fled to thy protection, implored thy help, or sought thine intercession was left unaided. Inspired with this**

confidence, I fly unto thee, O Virgin of virgins, my mother; to thee do I come, before thee I stand, sinful and sorrowful. O Mother of the Word Incarnate, despise not my petitions, but in thy mercy, hear and answer me. Amen.

You will notice in the first lines of the ***Memorare Prayer,*** at the end of the chaplet, I have added the words **"help me to remember."** I am sure that our Blessed Mother remembers how much she loves us and how well she responds to our needs, but this was added to **help us remember.**

What followed was my request that night and our Lady's response to my heart. In a little prayer, I asked her **if she didn't like** what I put together that she would send me a

red rose, and if **she liked it,** she would send me a **yellow one.**

Then I went to bed. The next morning, which, of course, was **the Feast of Our Lady of Lourdes,** I read the Office of Readings for the day in the Liturgy of the Hours, which I especially like to do on feast days.

In the account of our Lady's appearance to Saint Bernadette, I read this: *"Then I looked up and caught sight of the cave where I saw a lady wearing a lovely white dress with a bright belt. On top of each of her feet **was a pale yellow rose**, the same color as her rosary beads."*[5] That, I felt in my heart, **was our Lady's way of saying that she liked the chaplet.**

---

[5] Catholic Church, *The Liturgy of the hours: according to the Roman rite* (New York: Catholic Book Publishing Corp., 1976). Pg. 1673.

I have since shared that chaplet with a number of people in our parish, friends, and members of the clergy. The response I received was so positive that I introduced it as part of our devotions on the Feast of Divine Mercy and decided to incorporate it into my revised website, which was launched in June of 2017. God willing, it will be a blessing for you.

The URL is:
http://www.lifeinfocus.net/motherofmercychaplet.html

The picture which appears with this chaplet on my website was handed down to our family by my grandfather, Charles J. Neral, who came to America in 1905. It was on a

focus on the moment and trust in God's Love

holy card that his mother gave to him as she **entrusted him to the care of the Blessed Virgin Mary.**

In saying this chaplet, I pray that we too are entrusting ourselves to the merciful heart of our Blessed Mother.

8. A GIFT FROM SAINT THÉRÈSE

JMJ

During the season of Lent in 2016, I decided to reread the diary of Saint Maria Faustina, **Divine Mercy in My Soul,** from beginning to end, in preparation for Easter and the celebration of Divine Mercy Sunday. This was an amazingly rewarding experience. I was also introduced to another book that has helped to change my life. It is called **33 Days to Merciful Love,**[6] written by Fr. Michael E. Gaitley, MIC, a member of the **Congregation**

---

[6] Michael E. Gaitley, MIC. *33 Days to Merciful Love* (Stockbridge, MA: Marian Press, 2016).

of Marians, who run the ***Divine Mercy Center*** in Stockbridge, MA. It is a book designed to guide one on a thirty-three-day individual retreat in preparation for a ***Consecration to the Divine Mercy.*** One of the first things I discovered in the book is that Saint Thérèse of Lisieux, the Little Flower of Jesus, had a tremendous devotion to Jesus's Divine Mercy and wrote about **His Merciful Love** before Saint Maria Faustina was even born. It's certainly worth noting that Saint Thérèse was directed from the age of fourteen by Father Almire Pichon. He was a Jesuit, who was very familiar with the writings of Jean-Pierre de Caussade, also a Jesuit, who wrote the book I referenced earlier, ***Abandonment to Divine Providence.*** Is it any wonder that the teaching of that Jesuit priest filtered through to Saint Thérèse? That also helps to explain why confidence and abandonment, or trust, are keys words in her teachings.

I spent a week of the ***Thirty-three Days*** pondering the **faith and trust** of Abraham and our Blessed Mother, Mary. The second week I spent pondering how the faith of Abraham and Mary is mirrored in the faith and trust of Saint Thérèse as expressed in her **"*Little Way.*"** Week three was spent in thinking and praying about the ***Offering to Merciful Love,*** for which I was preparing. In the fourth week, I was reminded of how we all live in the reality of the darkness of sin. I also became more aware of the concept that those who approach God with all their heart and soul, mind, and will also experience a darkness of soul that can only be endured by the light of grace. Once I completed the book and made

the Consecration to Merciful Love, I needed to tell everyone about the experience.

The ***Feast of Divine Mercy*** seemed like the obvious opportunity to share with a large group of people the message which had touched my heart. In my homily that day, I introduced the congregation to the ***33 Days to Merciful Love*** retreat book. I then explained to them how I felt that Saint Maria Faustina, with her Diary, and Saint Thérèse had ganged up on me to further enlighten me regarding the profound mystery of God's Divine Mercy. I encouraged all of those who attended our devotions to read Fr. Michael Gaitley's book in preparation for a ***Consecration to Merciful Love.*** I also made a number of the books available, and, as I recall, our supply lasted only a few minutes after our service.

A Gift from Saint Thérèse

During the following week, I received an amazing gift. On the Friday after Divine Mercy Sunday, someone who was at that celebration at Saint Catherine of Siena Parish, in Duncansville, came to Saint John the Evangelist Parish in Altoona for Mass. After Mass, this person said, "I have something for you." Within minutes, I received a little box containing **a first-class relic of Saint Thérèse of Lisieux.** I was overwhelmed and have treasured that gift in my prayer corner at home ever since. Within a few weeks, I was also able to obtain a reliquary **that matches the one I had obtained, in 1999, for the first-class relic of Saint Maria Faustina.**

9. MORE GIFTS FROM OUR LADY AND SAINT JOSEPH

JMJ

Things happened pretty fast from then on. In the week after Divine Mercy Sunday in 2016, I also became aware of the book that Fr. Gaitley referred to at the beginning of his book on ***33 Days to Merciful Love;*** it is called ***33 Days to Morning Glory.***[7] In it, he recommends a way of preparing for a **Consecration to our Blessed Mother.** He actually recommends that people complete the

---

[7] Gaitley, Michael E. Gaitley, MIC. 2014. *33 Days to Morning Glory* (Stockbridge, MA: Marian Press, 2014).

book and the Consecration to Mary before the Consecration to the Divine Mercy. Within a couple weeks after that, I ordered another supply of both books and began to share them with anyone who would listen. I personally completed the book and the Consecration to our Blessed Mother. Since then, we have been able to introduce these gifts to many individuals. In fact, over two hundred books are in the hands of people interested in doing the retreats and the ***Consecration to our Immaculate Mother*** and to ***God's Merciful Love.***

In the process, I mentioned to my spiritual director, my pastor, and many others who would listen to me that those books and the consecration changed my life in many ways. **The Mass is different. The rosary**

is different because I now **think more of Mary as I say it,** and every day, I try to **walk and pray the Stations of the Cross with Mary.**

Amazingly, in the beginning of 2020, I discovered another book which has been a marvelous gift. It is entitled ***Consecration to St. Joseph,***[8] written by Very Rev. Donald W. Calloway, MIC, STL, Vicar Provincial of the Marians of the Immaculate Conception.

As I mentioned previously, upon graduation from grade school, in 1954, I spent almost five years with the **Society of Mary, *"Marianists."*** In his book on ***Consecration to St. Joseph,*** Fr. Calloway included many excerpts from Blessed William Joseph Chaminade, the founder of the ***Marianists.***

---

[8] Donald H. Calloway, MIC. *Consecration to St. Joseph* (Stockbridge, MA: Marian Press, 2020).

While I was with the ***Marianists,*** it didn't seem to register well enough, but now I know why every time we engaged in an activity in high school and college, we were encouraged to dedicate it to **"JMJ,"** Jesus, Mary, **and** Joseph. I also remember that every time Bishop Fulton J. Sheen wrote on his blackboard on the TV series, he wrote at the top "JMJ."

Remember, as I related in chapter three, my first visit to the hermitage, I was assigned to a cabin that was under ***the patronage of Saint Joseph.*** That was probably another indication that God wanted me to rely on the protection of Saint Joseph in my life, but I didn't get the full message at that time either.

However, for many years now, I have included in my Morning Prayer one which says:

"Eternal Father, You chose Saint Joseph to be the foster father of Jesus and the husband of Mary. Please grant that, through his intercession, I may be a better husband and father, a better grandfather, father-in-law, and a better deacon. You entrusted the needs of the family of Nazareth to Saint Joseph, so I entrust the needs of my family to him as well; that I may make decisions in line with what he would do. May I be a better worker, deacon, listener, and teacher; that I may be a better son, brother, and friend; that everything I say and everything I do will be for Your honor and glory and the salvation of souls, through Christ our Lord, Amen."

After spending the Thirty-Three Days with the period of preparation, I have now consecrated my life to Saint Joseph on his Feast day on March 19th and renewed it on the Feast of Saint Joseph the Worker on May 1st. From now on, I dedicate everything I say and everything I do to Jesus, Mary, and St. Joseph.

In just a few short weeks, I have been able to introduce over forty people to the idea of ***Consecration to Saint Joseph,*** and I am in awe of the number of those who are so anxious to know more about and devote themselves more fully to Saint Joseph.

I shall ever be grateful for these moments of grace in my life.

10. FEEDBACK FROM THOSE CARDS

> JMJ

When I first started handing out the *"focus"* cards, as I mentioned earlier, I didn't really understand the true meaning of the words. I kept emphasizing the word *"focus"* in my explanation of it. It wasn't until after my discussion with my spiritual director in 1995 that I began to use the phrase which I mentioned in Chapter 4: ***"Read it forward; live it backwards."***

In the twenty-nine-plus years of giving my little card to thousands of people and eventually learning how to properly explain it, the response has far exceeded my expectations. One of the classic responses has been, "I needed that." Another is, "I like that!" I have often had someone tell me, "I will keep that right here on my desk." Or upon visiting a person who is hospitalized or home-bound, they have said, "I will keep it right here on my nightstand."

Even more rewarding are the times when I meet someone or when a person walks up to me, and even before I have a chance to say hello, they say something like, ***"Your card is right by my bed,"*** or, ***"It** (your card) **is on my refrigerator door,"*** or, ***"Your card is next to my computer."***

I returned one day to a retreat center where I had been approximately eight years before.

focus on the moment and trust in God's Love

As soon as I walked into the office, I noticed that little card on the front of the desk of the receptionist. She said, ***"I look at it all the time, and it helps me to keep my focus."***

Quite a few years ago, a woman told me that she even took that card with her into the delivery room when she was about to have her baby. She said that every time things started to get really rough, she would look at the card and remember that she had to trust in God's love. Her son was born and is now a well-respected young man in our town.

Another woman, named Karen, came up to me after Mass one Sunday and told me that the card I had given her was getting handled too much and it had started to look a little shabby. She asked if she could have a new one. I cheerfully handed her another card when she gave me her tattered one. She signed the back of that card, ***"With love and appreciation, Karen."*** That shabby little card has been in my prayer corner at home for a number of years now. As far as I am concerned, it will always remain there as a reminder of her affirmation of its value.

One of my favorite recollections goes back to the funeral of a friend, Msgr. John J. Little, who died on December 30, 2005. As a member of the Diaconate community of our diocese, I was invited to participate in his Funeral Mass. There were so many priests and deacons looking for a place to vest for the Mass in the rectory, that his brother, Msgr. Anthony Little, suggested that we use Msgr. John's office.

focus on the moment and trust in God's Love

When I walked into that office, the first thing that caught my eyes was one of my little cards in the center of Msgr. John's desk. I picked up the card, showed it to his brother, and told him that I would really like him to keep it. He replied, ***"No, you should keep it because you know where it came from."*** I quickly agreed, and that card has also been in my prayer corner since that day, along with a remembrance card with Msgr. John's picture on it. By the way, I also gave Msgr. Anthony one of my cards, which, he recently assured me, he still has.

Another memorable response came from someone I never met. In July of 1999, I had the opportunity to spend a week on retreat at ***The Abbey of the Genesee*** in Genesee, New York. It is the home of a Roman Catholic community of contemplative monks who are part of a worldwide ***Order of Cistercians of the Strict Observance (O.C.S.O.),*** more commonly known as ***Trappists.***

In the course of my retreat, I met a religious brother from the ***Community of Franciscan Friars of the Renewal,*** founded by Fr. Benedict J. Groeschel, CFR. Brother Leo and I had the opportunity to talk during one of our leisure times. Of course, I seized the chance to share my little card with someone who I thought would really appreciate it.

To my surprise, several weeks later, I received a little note from Brother Leo. It read:

Dear Deacon Gene,

May the peace of Jesus Christ be with you! Last Saturday, I had the

focus on the moment and trust in God's Love

opportunity to share your story with Father Benedict as you related it to me at Genesee.

Your motto, *"focus on the moment and trust in God's love,"* **he said was true abandonment.**

Enclosed are a few things he asked to be mailed to you.

May God continue to bless you, your family, and your ministry. Let us pray for each other.

Brother Leo

Brother Leo sent me an autographed copy of a book Fr. Benedict wrote in 1995 called ***Arise from Darkness.***[9] Also included was

---

[9] Benedict J. Groeschel, CFR. *Arise from Darkness* (San Francisco, CA: Ignatius Press, 1995).

a set of cassette tapes called ***A Spirituality of Acceptance and Peace,*** a recording of a talk Fr. Benedict gave on Jean-Pierre de Caussade, the author of ***Abandonment to Divine Providence,*** the book which I referred to earlier and which had a profound effect on my life. And finally, there was a tape of a talk Fr. Benedict gave on ***the life of Saint Thérèse of Lisieux***. Needless to say, I was overwhelmed by that response from someone I had never met, but whom I very highly respected. All three of those gifts have contributed to my better understanding of God's work in my life.

Many of the thousands of those little cards that were given to people over the years may not still be on nightstands, refrigerators, or on computers. But regardless of where they are, I hope and pray that some benefit has been received because of them.

To be able to share my message with as many people as I could ever dream of doing one on one, I also decided to build a website on which I could introduce people to my ministry as a deacon and introduce them to this book.

Since you have the book and may not have seen the website, you can access it by using your computer, your tablet, or your cell phone.

The URL: www.lifeinfocus.net

CONCLUSION

JMJ

In these chapters, I have tried to explain something which had eluded me for many years and which still causes me to stand in awe of God's Love and Divine Providence.

Sometimes we don't appreciate our opportunities or we don't feel appreciated by circumstances, situations, and personal encounters that are presented to us during our busy day. How often do we encounter a situation or an individual who challenges us to use all the resources at our disposal to complete a task satisfactorily and to maintain

focus on the moment and trust in God's Love

---

our cool? Whether it is an emergency or a request from our children, our spouse, or our boss, we owe it to ourselves to do our best.

I have often told people, "If you focus on the moment and do your best, God will do the rest." God knows that even our best efforts will not be sufficient to create ***His masterpiece.*** Do we even understand what God is doing in our life right now? No! But, if we allow Him to do it, we are allowing Him to complete another step in His vision for our life. He wants us to accept the grace and to do the best we can with each moment as He gives it to us.

Why don't we do our best and trust that God will do the rest?

One of the most common problems that could cause us to **NOT** do our best is that we feel that our present task is insignificant in the big picture.

The fact is, with every breath we take, we are given another opportunity to be ourselves in the best way we can. We can use that moment for good, or we can let it pass with little consideration and never again receive that exact gift of grace.

It's much like painting a picture. The artist can place each stroke to the best of his or her ability and end up with a masterpiece. A "potential" artist can also putter around and end up with what looks like the dabbling of a child at play.

We need to ask ourselves this simple question:

"When I get to the end of this journey of life, do I want to be able to look back on my

focus on the moment and trust in God's Love

life and see God's masterpiece, or would I be satisfied to see a picture that looks like an incomplete work?"

If you would prefer the first option, you will probably need to use every color on your palate and give your best at every moment to make sure that your contributions to the big picture are your best efforts to allow God to create His masterpiece.

In the spring of 1997, the members of Saint John the Evangelist Parish, Lakemont, Altoona, Pennsylvania, had an experience that I hope will help to summarize all that has been said in these pages. We had the privilege of **watching** a master artist create a mural on the back wall of our new church. The mural took shape over the course of almost two years.

Conclusion

Unlike many artists who want to keep their work hidden until it is finished, this artist, Allen Michael Capriotti, allowed us to follow every step of the process. Week by week, we watched as the barren canvas began to bear the marks of a skilled craftsman at work. First, the fine strokes of the pencil, then the tint of the initial coat of glaze, followed by the first bursts of color as the mural began to come to life. Finally, the last coat of glaze brought out its real beauty. That amazing process requires that the artist has the picture in his mind before he starts. Can you imagine having an image in your mind and then spending two years putting it on canvas?

What we ended up seeing is a life-size painting of Jesus and His Apostles, with Martha and

focus on the moment and trust in God's Love

Mary, at the Raising of Lazarus as recorded in the Gospel of John 11:41–44.

One day, as I pondered that beautiful finished work, I began to ask myself if our life could be compared to that canvas. Just as our artist had that picture in his mind before he even started to work on the canvas, God had a picture of our life in His mind even before we were born.

Each moment of our life, God makes another mark on the canvas of our time on this earth. If we fail to respond to the work of His hands, those marks may just turn out to look like the dabbling of a child at play. But, if we allow the Lord to work in ***His way*** and ***TRUST*** that God knows what is best to complete the picture, the final image created by our life can be ***His masterpiece.***

Conclusion

God willing, through the guidance of **His Divine Providence,** some of these thoughts and insights will help you to respond to the work of **THE Master's hand.**

Simply put:

"focus and trust are brushes with which we allow God to make of our life His masterpiece."

Remember:

focus on the moment
and
trust in God's love

Read it forwards, live it backwards.
Believe that God loves me.
Then TRUST God with everything I am
and everything I have.
Then, and only then,
can I *focus on the moment,*
do my best, and
trust **that** *GOD*
will do the rest.

BIBLIOGRAPHY

Calloway, Donald H., MIC. *Consecration to St. Joseph.* Stockbridge, MA: Marian Press, 2020.

Catholic Church. *The Liturgy of the hours: according to the Roman rite.* (New York: Catholic Book Publishing Corp., 1976. Pg. 1673.

de Caussade, Jean-Pierre. *Abandonment to Divine Providence.* New York: Doubleday, 1975.

Gaitley, Michael E., MIC. *33 Days to Morning Glory.* Stockbridge, MA: Marian Press, 2014.

Gaitley, Michael E., MIC. *33 Days to Merciful Love.* Stockbridge, MA: Marian Press, 2016.

Groeschel, Benedict J., CFR. *Arise from Darkness.* San Francisco, CA: Ignatius Press, 1995.

Hurd, Robert. *Breaking Bread.* "*Transfigure Us, O Lord.*" Portland: OCP, 2020. #499.

Kowalska, M. Faustina, SMDM. *The Diary of the Servant of God Sister M. Faustina Kowalska: Divine Mercy in My Soul.* Stockbridge, MA: Marian Press, 1987.

Thérèse. *Story of a Soul: the autobiography of St. Therese of Lisieux.* (London: Burns, Oats & Washbourne, 1912. Pg. 203.

www.ingramcontent.com/pod-product-compliance
Lightning Source LLC
LaVergne TN
LVHW042246070526
838201LV00089B/40